Historical
AMERICA

Historical
AMERICA

The Northwestern States

by
D. J. Herda

The Millbrook Press
Brookfield, Connecticut
The American Scene

Cover photos courtesy of (clockwise from top left)
Library of Congress (2), D. J. Herda

Photos courtesy of the Library of Congress: pp. 8, 11, 18,
20, 27, 36, 43, 47; Alaska Division of Tourism: pp. 16, 51;
The Granger Collection: p. 23; D. J. Herda: pp. 30, 33, 41, 54.

Library of Congress Cataloging-in-Publication Data

Herda, D. J., 1948–
Historical America. The northwestern states / by D. J. Herda.
p.   cm. — (The American scene)
Includes bibliographical references and index.
Summary: Examines the history of the northwestern states and
Alaska, from early Indian civilizations through colonization and
exploitation to the present day.
ISBN 1-56294-122-4 (lib. bdg.)
1. Northwestern States—History—Juvenile literature.   2. Alaska—
History—Juvenile literature.   [1. Northwestern States—History.
2. Alaska—History.]   I. Title.   II. Series.
F597.H53   1993
979.5—dc20   92-16312   CIP   AC

Published by The Millbrook Press
2 Old New Milford Road
Brookfield, Connecticut 06804

CONTENTS

INTRODUCTION

Historical America: The Northwestern States traces the development of the northwestern United States, from the earliest Indian inhabitants through the statehood years, a span of more than a century. The region made up of Montana, Wyoming, Idaho, Oregon, Washington, and Alaska has played an exciting role in the history of the United States.

One of the last regions of the country to be settled by white Americans, the Northwest has long been home to many Native American cultures—from the ancient Tlingit and Haida tribes of Alaska to the more recent Plains Indians of Montana and Wyoming.

Despite the early expeditions of English, French, Russian, and Spanish explorers, the region remained largely unsettled by white Americans until well into the 1800s. The Spanish conquistadors had explored and settled much of the Southwest; the American Revolution had come and gone in the East; the Civil War had taken its deadly toll in the South; and European immigrants had already moved into the north central United States before the first transcontinental railroads began bringing Americans by the carloads to the Northwest.

France did not give up its hold over the Louisiana Territory, which included parts of present-day Montana and Wyoming, until the Louisiana Purchase of 1803. Great Britain did not surrender its holdings in the vast Oregon Territory until a treaty fixed the U.S.–Canadian border at its present location in 1846. Russia did not give up its claim to Alaska until 1867, when the United States purchased the last of Russia's holdings there for $7.2 million.

Yet today, there is remarkably little evidence of these foreign powers, except for some Russian architecture and traditions in Alaska. Instead, the people of the Northwest tend to be rugged, free-spirited, pioneering Americans.

THE INDIANS OF THE NORTHWEST

Over the years, Hollywood has painted a picture of the American Indian as a red-skinned brave with a brilliantly painted face, flowing robes, and a war bonnet made of eagle feathers. Movies and television have portrayed him riding across the wide-open plains on a sleek, fast horse in constant search of a wagon train of white settlers on which to prey.

This was not the real Plains Indian. Until well into the 1800s, the Plains Indians lived simple lives in peace with most of their neighbors. They traveled on foot in their search for food—just as their ancestors had done for thousands of years.

THE HORSE COMES TO THE PLAINS

The Indians of the plains had never seen a horse before the Spanish brought the animal to New Mexico in 1598. The Spanish government had prohibited selling horses to the natives, but the Pueblo Indians raided a Spanish camp in 1680 and captured most of the Spaniards' herd. The Spaniards quickly rebuilt their herds, but they were unable to halt the frequent raids by the Pueblo Indians and other southwestern tribes. Before long, numerous groups of Indians had built up their own herds of horses and began trading them to neighboring tribes. Some Indians made a profitable business from stealing horses, which they then sold to those northern tribes that hadn't yet acquired them. Some horses escaped and roamed wild over the plains—free for any tribes able to capture and break them. The Spanish called these horses *mestengos*, meaning wild, from which the English word mustangs comes.

By 1750 a new way of life for the Plains Indians had evolved as horse trading spread throughout the West. The animals—as

(opposite page)
"Encampment of Piekann Indians near Fort McKenzie on the Musselshell River," 1842, by Rice & Clark. Plains tribes often lived in tepees—conical structures made of animal skins stretched over wooden frames.

well as the knowledge of how to break and train them—quickly traveled northward from New Mexico into the present-day states of Colorado, Utah, and Montana. Throughout the first half of the eighteenth century, Indian merchants were selling horses to the northern Shoshoni, who lived in present-day northern Utah and Idaho. The Shoshoni gradually built up their herds and were soon riding as if they had been born on horseback.

Once a poor, peaceful tribe of farmers at the mercy of their stronger neighbors, the Shoshoni learned to use the horse to great advantage. From their home in the Rocky Mountains, the tribe could swoop down the eastern flanks of the range onto the plains where they discovered more bison (or buffalo) than they had ever dreamed existed. They also discovered that the Blackfoot, who had not yet acquired horses, were no longer the feared enemy that they once were.

As word of the magnificent horse spread, Indian groups from around the country flocked to the plains in search of the prized animal. The Athapaskan (Kiowa Apache) came from the north; the Algonquian (Cree, Cheyenne, and Blackfoot) and the Siouan (Mandan, Crow, and Dakota) from the east; the Uto-Aztecan (Comanche and Ute) from the west; and the Caddoan (Pawnee and Arikara) from the south. With horses, the once-peaceful tribes of farmers and hunters changed into feared and respected warriors. Their economies changed, too. Now the world of the Plains Indian revolved not around day-to-day survival, but around the abundance of the American bison. In the past, Indians could get close enough to kill only the weakest or sickest of animals. These they took back to their camp to use for food and raw materials—hooves, horns, and bones for tools, tendons for string, and hides for clothing. Nothing went to waste, for no one knew when another bison might fall to the hunter's bow or spear.

Once mounted, though, the Plains Indians were more than a match for even the youngest, strongest, and fastest of bison. For the first time in history, Indians were killing more bison than they needed for their own survival. They began trading the excess skins and dried meat—called jerky—to those tribes that had not yet obtained horses. They even traded some bison

to whites, who made a fortune shipping the meat and skins back East, where bison was highly prized as a delicacy.

By the early 1800s, an era in Indian history had come to an end as every tribe on the plains rushed to acquire the horses it needed to compete for food and to protect itself from raids by neighboring tribes. But within a matter of a few short years, another era would be ushered in. And it would have far more serious consequences for the Plains Indian than anyone could ever have imagined.

An Indian on horseback races after a bison on the Great Plains in the 1820s.

THE PLAINS INDIANS DISCOVER GUNS

By 1800 some Plains tribes had begun acquiring guns by trading furs to the Hudson's Bay Company and other English trading companies in the region. The Indians had watched white men use guns for years and were quick to realize their power and versatility on the plains. Guns quickly became the most prized objects in the white trader's stock of supplies.

At first, the Indians used these "talking sticks," as they were called, for hunting. No longer did a brave need to ride to within ten or fifteen feet of a bison to kill it with a spear or a bow and arrow. Now he could bring down an animal four times his size with a single shot from fifty yards away. But before long, the Indians learned that guns could be used for other purposes. A handful of trained marksmen with guns were worth dozens of conventionally armed braves in battle. In time, several northwestern tribes began expanding their territorial range, seeking new enemies to conquer.

The Blackfoot tribes of Montana were among the earliest Plains Indians to acquire guns. The Salish tribes west and south of them, on the other hand, had no guns, so the Blackfoot raided them constantly. When white traders attempted to carry a supply of guns across the mountains to trade to the Salish, the Blackfoot forcibly turned them back. As long as they could prevent the Salish from obtaining weapons, the Blackfoot would dominate the region.

But, although guns were a great asset to the Indian, they had their disadvantages. Indians had not learned to make or repair guns or to manufacture gunpowder. And without gunpowder, guns were useless. If a gun happened to break down in the middle of a battle, the brave who held it was helpless.

The Plains Indians learned this lesson the hard way, as had other Indians before them. As early as 1691, the Mohawk tribe on the Atlantic Coast had petitioned the Council at Albany for a gunsmith to live among the tribe. "Wee begge of you to let us have a smith and a gunn stock maker in our [tribe] to mend our armes [guns] when they are broken."[1]

The Indians of the plains discovered quickly that they could acquire hundreds of guns, learn to shoot them with deadly accuracy, and still be at a disadvantage in a battle with whites, who were steadily moving westward onto Indian land. The Indians realized that their dependence upon whites for both guns and gunpowder made them in effect the slaves, while the whites—who controlled the supply of these goods—had become the masters. But they had no alternative. They were forced to labor in the forest, trapping and killing animals to obtain the furs they needed to trade with whites for guns and ammunition.

Meanwhile, the white traders who provided the Indians with guns and gunpowder realized this, too. No matter how many arms they traded to the Indians, the Indians would always remain at a disadvantage. And the whites would continue growing wealthy from their furs.

So the Plains Indians by the mid-1800s had reached a plateau. Horses and guns had provided them with new economic and cultural opportunities. They also increased the frequency and deadliness of Indian battles on the plains. As more white Americans traveled west in search of new land and wealth from gold, silver, and other minerals that lay in the ground, conflicts with the Indians inevitably arose. As battles broke out, the U.S. government sent soldiers to build forts and scour the countryside for signs of renegade tribes.

Yet, despite all of the forts, all of the soldiers, and all of the promises that the government made to the Indians and ultimately broke, there was remarkably little combat. The Plains Indians experienced years of death and hardship at the hands of whites, but most of their problems were caused by starvation, exposure, disease, and alcoholism—not by bullets. Far more damage was done to the Plains Indians by greedy, thoughtless, or cruel whites who tricked or forced Indians off their lands and very nearly exterminated the American bison. In the process, they destroyed the Plains Indians' main source of food. Without food, there could be no Plains Indians. And without Plains Indians, the last stumbling block to the West with all of its wealth and resources would be gone forever.

THE INDIANS OF THE COAST

The Plains Indians occupied most of the flatlands east of the Rocky Mountains. Few tribes lived among the mountains, which the Indians found to be too hot and dry in summer and too cold and snowy in winter. But west of the Rockies, where the land flattens out into plains that run to the foothills of the Cascade Mountains, lived a group of Indians called the Plateau peoples. They included the Nez Percé, Spokan, Colville, Okanogan, Yakima, Wenatchee, and Cayuse. They, like the Plains Indians to the east, were excellent horse people. Most of the Plateau people lived in the fertile valleys between the Rockies and the Cascades.

West of the Cascades lived another group called the Northwest Coast Indians, which included the Puyallup, Nisqualli, Clallam, Chinook, Clatsop, and Nooksack tribes. Their lands ranged from the inland mountains to the mighty Pacific Ocean. Unlike some Indian tribes, they were blessed with a wealth of natural game. Each spring, the rivers of the region were swollen with millions of huge spawning salmon coming upstream from the ocean to lay their eggs. Sometimes, the salmon ran so heavily that the fish could be scooped out of the shallower waters by hand. When the Indians tired of eating salmon, there was plenty of other food available—halibut and whale in the ocean and deer, elk, roots, and berries in the forests.

For shelter, these northwest fishermen were equally blessed. The giant red cedar that dominated the forests from northern California north to central Alaska grew so straight and tall and produced such soft wood that the Indians were able to cut the trees easily and carve them with simple hand tools. They used wooden wedges to split the trunks into rough planks, then tied the planks to posts with vines in order to make long, barnlike structures. Some of these buildings housed as many as eight or ten different Indian families.

The Indians also found red cedar to be an ideal material for making eating utensils such as dishes and spoons. They made small ornate boxes by steaming pieces of cedar until they could be bent into shape and held together with vines. They would sometimes paint images on the boxes with dyes made from native plants.

Red cedar proved useful in making clothing, too. The women beat the bark against a rock until it separated into soft threads. They then wove these threads into short fringed skirts.

The cedar trees also provided the tribes with material from which to build canoes. Long, thin boats—called dugout canoes—were made by charring the inside of a tree trunk with a torch. Then the charred wood was scraped out with a knife made of stone or the bone of some animal. The tribes made different canoes for different purposes. Some were built for paddling on inland lakes and rivers. Some were used for fishing or warfare. Still others, measuring 30 feet or more, were stable enough to ride the waves of the Pacific Ocean without capsizing. These ocean-going canoes proved especially useful to the tribes that relied on whale blubber for food.

THE NATIVES OF ALASKA

Far to the north of the Pacific coast and Oregon lies a sprawling land that is still largely undeveloped. The land is called Alaska. Here, vast herds of elk, musk oxen, and caribou roam the countryside. Whales, seals, salmon, otters, and sea lions swim the oceans. Huge polar bears—the largest flesh-eating animals on earth—roam the massive ice fields in their endless search for food.

It is here, too, that the native Eskimos (or Inuit) and Aleut live. Like all Native Americans, they were descended from Asian people. Along with the two groups lived the two largest Alaskan Indian tribes, the Tlingit and Haida. Most of these Native Alaskans were peaceful, although some skirmishes broke out between the Tlingit and the Russian traders who had set up large trading and fishing outposts in the region.

The first Americans to visit the area came aboard a whaling ship in 1848. The ship had traveled from New York through the Bering Strait and into the Arctic Ocean. Before long, other ships joined it. Within a matter of a few years, more than 250 vessels regularly cruised the icy shores of Alaska in search of whales.

The whalers brought disaster to the Native Alaskans. They introduced the Tlingit and Haida to hard liquor, and drunkenness soon became a major problem. In 1874, Ivan Petroff,

Haidas carve a totem pole today in Haines, Alaska, as they have for centuries. These carved poles represent tribes and families.

Alaska's first census taker, detailed the seriousness of the problem: "Living directly in the track of vessels bound for the Arctic for the purpose of whaling and trading, this situation has been a curse to them [the Native Alaskans]; for as long as the rum lasts, they do nothing but drink and fight among themselves."[2]

Worse still, the whalers soon began depleting the supply of bowhead whales and walrus, which the natives relied on for survival. Between 1860 and 1880, the number of walrus killed by whalers reached 200,000. Before long, many Native Alaskans were unable to find enough food. Their tribes grew weak and even more susceptible to disease. Many natives died of starvation and malnutrition.

Other whites created even more serious problems for the Native Alaskans. In the spring of 1880, a U.S. Navy commander sent a group of prospectors into the Chilkat village to search for gold. The Chilkat had a long history of trading with the various tribes of Alaska's interior. Although the Americans failed to find gold, they had succeeded in opening up Alaska to white exploration and settlement. The region would never again be the same.

CHAPTER TWO

WESTWARD HO!

In the first decades of the 1800s, the United States extended west only as far as the Rocky Mountains. Both Great Britain and America claimed the northwestern land that lay between the Rockies and the Pacific Ocean. But very few people from either country lived there. Although Meriwether Lewis and William Clark had explored the region as early as 1805, most of the area's residents were either Indians or French Canadian trappers and traders. The land to the south, including California, still belonged to Mexico.

Meanwhile, the fur trade was opening up the Northwest along the shores of the Missouri River. In 1822, Missouri businessman William H. Ashley sent his first trading party to the Northwest. Three years later, Ashley developed the "rendezvous system" of trading, in which trappers, traders, and Indians from all over Rocky Mountain country met once a year at a designated place. Usually this was in the Grand Teton Mountains.

But by 1840, the enormous profit from fur trading had dried up. The streams no longer teemed with beaver. The country was trapped out. The few remaining animals were saved from extinction only by changing fashions. Beaver hats, which had once been the rage in the eastern United States and Europe, had been replaced by silk. There was no longer much call for beaver skins.

The glory years of the fur industry had helped to open up the Northwest to exploration and settlement. The trade had attracted a unique group of reckless adventurers known as "mountain men." These men left the comforts of city life for the call of the wilderness. Often they lived in total isolation, sometimes in forts, occasionally among the Indians. Men such as Jim Bridger, Kit Carson, and Jim Beckwourth were the first whites to find their way across the Rocky Mountains. They

(opposite page)
"The Unknown Explorers," by Frederic Remington. In the early 1800s the Northwest region was a vast wilderness, explored only by seasoned, adventurous trappers.

were the first to pioneer trails into Oregon Country, an enormous stretch of land that included the present-day states of Oregon, Washington, Idaho, and parts of Montana and Wyoming, as well as western Canada.[1]

This engraving shows Kit Carson with a group of fur trappers. After exploring the Southwest, he headed north to the Rockies. His mapmaker created the first accurate map of the West.

The actual settlement of Oregon Country by white Americans began in 1834, when a group of American missionaries traveled west. The Methodist Missionary Society led by the Reverend Jason Lee came to Oregon to bring Christianity to the Indians. Guided by fur traders and mountain men, Lee settled in the scenic Willamette Valley. Two years later, Marcus and Narcissa Whitman established a second mission near Fort

Walla Walla in present-day Washington. Other missionaries soon followed.

Although these missionaries failed to convert many Indians to Christianity, they sent glowing reports about the beauty of Oregon Country back to the East. When the missionaries returned east to raise money for their religious work, they gave speeches about the new Northwest. They told stories about the rich farmland and bountiful waters off the Oregon coast. They amazed their listeners with tales of wild animals and mild climates.

Before long, a small group of farm families followed the trail toward Oregon. In 1843 a larger group made up of nearly a thousand settlers gathered at Independence, Missouri, the closest large town, for the long trip west. Marcus Whitman himself, on his return from the East, served as the group's guide. During the next few years, thousands of additional settlers moved into Oregon Country.

THE BIRTH OF MANIFEST DESTINY

By the mid-1840s, Americans were beginning to think that the United States should extend from the Atlantic to the Pacific oceans. In 1845 editor John Louis O'Sullivan wrote in the *United States Magazine and Democratic Review*, "Our manifest destiny is to overspread the continent allotted by Providence for the free development of our yearly multiplying millions."

Other magazine and newspaper editors picked up O'Sullivan's words, and before long, the term "manifest destiny" had become a common phrase in the American press. It represented the way most Americans of the day thought—that it was their right to settle all of the land between the two coasts. One of the greatest stretches of unsettled land in the mid-1800s was Oregon Country.

As the idea of manifest destiny grew in popularity across the nation, more and more Americans moved west. By 1846 more than five thousand people were living in Oregon.

But Oregon was not yet an American territory. It was still claimed by Great Britain. For a while, it looked as if the two countries might go to war over ownership of the region. Then, in 1846, the United States and Great Britain reached an agreement. They would divide the Oregon Country at the 49th parallel of latitude. All land north of that line would belong to Great Britain. All land to the south would belong to the United States. To this day, that line serves as the boundary between the United States and Canada.

A LONG AND DANGEROUS JOURNEY

For the American pioneer families who chose to make the two-thousand-mile trip to Oregon, the journey was both long and dangerous. When the time neared to begin the trip, the families would gather at Independence, Missouri, and choose a leader and guide. Then they would form their wagons into two columns and set off along the Oregon Trail to the wagonmaster's call of "Westward Ho!"

In the first column were the families that had no livestock or, at most, just a few animals. Behind them was the "cow column," which was made up of families bringing a large number of cattle, horses, and oxen. Some wagon trains included more than two hundred wagons, stretching out along the plains for more than a mile.

The first part of the journey took the wagon train across the Great Plains, where for hundreds of miles the pioneers saw little besides open grassland. The guide rode ahead to look for fresh water, scout out camping sites, and keep a watchful eye for hostile Indians.

The train would stop an hour or so before sunset to allow the pioneers time to make camp. After a long day on the trail, most people were settled into bed by 7 or 8 P.M. The next day began at 4 A.M. After breakfast, the children milked the cows and helped their parents take down the tents. Then all the family's belongings had to be reloaded in the wagons. The oxen and horses were hitched up, and the train was rolling along the trail again by 7 A.M.

In order to lighten the load, only mothers with small children and the sick or injured rode in the wagons. The men usually rode horseback, acting as guards against possible Indian attacks and sometimes leaving the trail to hunt game for the evening meal. Everyone else walked alongside the wagons. By sunset, the drivers would pull the wagons into a circle into

which the animals were herded to prevent them from wandering off during the night.

Although some days went smoothly, they were the exception rather than the rule. Many unexpected problems arose along the trail. Wagon wheels shattered from the heavy loads, axles broke in two, animals drank spoiled water and got sick or died, and food and other provisions ran low. The relentless summer sun baked the earthen trail dry, and great clouds of dust kicked high up into the air. Within minutes, a sudden rainstorm could turn the earth into thick, sticky mud. Still, the train had to keep rolling. The wagons had to pass through the high mountain passes before the heavy snows came in the fall, or the travelers would be stranded.

After crossing the Rocky Mountains through the South Pass,

Oxen strain against heavy loads, as a covered wagon train makes its way west on the Oregon Trail.

23

the pioneers were greeted by a welcome sight—Fort Bridger. The fort was actually a small rest stop built by the fabled mountain man and guide Jim Bridger. There the families could get clean water for themselves and fresh food for their animals.

After a short stopover, the travelers were on their way again. Ahead of them lay the rugged western slope of the South Pass. The wagons had to move slowly to keep from tumbling down into the valley. Many families were forced to lighten their loads by throwing away some of their furniture and other belongings. The trail was soon strewn with once-cherished items that sat decaying in the sun.

Once through the pass, the settlers traveled across parts of Idaho and through the Blue Mountains before finally swinging south along the banks of the Columbia River to a broad, fertile valley called the Willamette. Its sweeping green meadows and gently rolling slopes must have looked like heaven after the grueling six-month trip. It was here that most of the thousands of settlers who first came to Oregon Country made their homes.

PROBLEMS ON THE PLAINS

By the late 1800s, the growing number of settlers on the western plains was beginning to threaten the life-style of the area's Indians. Before the Civil War, many white Americans thought of the Northwest as an empty, barren land. But pioneers crossing the plains on their way to Oregon Country soon learned differently. This was the land of the Plains Indians, who had lived there for centuries. They had been guaranteed exclusive hunting rights to the land in various treaties made with them by the U.S. government. In return, the Indians promised not to attack passing wagon trains.

But soon the growing number of settlers in the area changed all that. Whites began hunting the bison upon which the Indians relied for food, clothing, and shelter. The settlers built cabins on Indian land and began grazing cattle on the open grasslands. Gold strikes throughout the Northwest brought miners and prospectors flocking to the area. Small settlements sprang up almost overnight. Many of them grew quickly into towns. When the Indians complained that the government was failing to honor its part of the treaty, the government ignored them. Finally, the Indians decided to act.

By the late 1860s, armed bands of Indians swept down from the mountains to attack white settlements on the western plains. They burned farmhouses and barns, stole or slaughtered cattle, and destroyed settlers' crops. To protect the settlers from the Indians, the U.S. government was called upon to send troops into the area. Large numbers of mounted soldiers—pony soldiers, the Indians called them—served only to worsen the situation. Between 1868 and 1875, more than two hundred battles were fought between the Indians and U.S. government soldiers along the western frontier.[2] Meanwhile, farther west along the Pacific Coast, new hostilities were preparing to erupt.

THE MODOC WARS

By the mid-1800s, the land surrounding the mouth of the Columbia River in Oregon Country had been only sparsely settled by white Americans. The area did not begin to flourish until Spain, Russia, and Great Britain gave up their claims to the region. Finally, in 1846, the United States became the sole possessor of the area, which included most of the present-day Northwest.

When Congress declared Oregon an official U.S. territory in 1848, Americans curious about the region began flooding the area. By 1859, enough people lived in the territory to qualify it to enter the Union as the 33rd state.

Although most of the Pacific Coastal tribes had been peaceful toward their new neighbors, one—the Modoc of southern Oregon—won a unique place in the history of the region. In 1864, the Modoc agreed to surrender their land to the U.S. government and were moved to the Klamath Reservation in southern Oregon. The Klamath Indians and the Modoc had long been bitter rivals, however, and neither tribe enjoyed sharing its land with the other. Finally, in 1870, the Modoc left the reservation to return to the land that had long belonged to their ancestors.

In 1872, the U.S. government ordered the tribe back to the reservation. The Modoc flatly refused and, under the leadership of their chief, Captain Jack, fought off a detachment of soldiers sent out to retrieve them. The tribe went on a rampage, attacking white settlements, killing settlers, and burning buildings. Then they retreated to the safety of the rugged country known as the Lava Beds along the border between southern Oregon and northern California.

The Lava Beds proved to be an ideal place for the Modoc to make their stand against the army. When a small body of troops was sent against them, the Modoc easily defeated the soldiers and disappeared into the rugged terrain. The government responded by sending a group of mediators out to attempt to settle the conflict peacefully, but one group of Modoc warriors made the fateful mistake of killing the representatives. Within weeks, the government launched a full-scale military campaign against the Indians.

For a while, the Modoc managed to elude their pursuers. But eventually, a group of the tribe's best braves was surrounded and killed. Eventually, Captain Jack and several other leaders were cornered in a cave and forced to surrender. At the trial that followed, Captain Jack and three other Modoc leaders were sentenced to hang. They were executed on October 3, 1873. The surviving Modoc were sent to the Quapaw Reservation in Indian Territory in Oklahoma.

Several other Indian tribes tried to resist the military power of the advancing whites, but they, too, met with disaster. By 1875, most of the northwestern tribes had been forced onto reservations. It was only a matter of time before the Pacific Northwest would be open at last to unrestricted settlement.

THE BATTLE OF LITTLE BIGHORN

Meanwhile, in 1868, the U.S. government had just signed a treaty with the Sioux. The treaty called for the Sioux to settle within the Black Hills Reservation in Dakota Territory. But by 1874, trouble had erupted.

Lieutenant Colonel George Armstrong Custer had recently led an expedition into the Black Hills of South Dakota. Custer returned with tales of large amounts of gold just waiting to be taken. Before long, the reservation was crawling with prospectors anxious to strike it rich. To help control the rush and to

prevent still more violations of the treaty that prohibited whites from trespassing on reservation land, the government called in the U.S. Army.

But the soldiers were nearly powerless to stem the flow of the thousands of easterners who were flooding the area with hopes of finding overnight wealth. Finally, a large number of Sioux warriors decided to take matters into their own hands. A band of angry young braves left the reservation to join a group of Cheyenne gathered at the Little Bighorn River in southern Montana. The chief of the group was Crazy Horse, a powerful Sioux warrior who was determined to stop the advancing whites at any cost.

Even though the Sioux and their Cheyenne allies defeated Custer and his men at the Battle of Little Bighorn, this momentary triumph spelled disaster for the Indians.

27

When word that the Indians were on the move reached the soldiers, the army struck hard and fast. After several encounters with scattered bands of Sioux warriors and a few small hunting parties, Custer stumbled upon the main camp of the Sioux and their Cheyenne allies on the banks of the Little Bighorn River. Custer received word to wait for reinforcements. But he was a headstrong and brash leader who did not want to share the glory of capturing Crazy Horse and Sitting Bull, another powerful Sioux chief, with anyone. In a fatal mistake, Custer ordered his detachment of soldiers to split into two main groups. He led his group into the Indians' camp, which numbered more than 2,500 braves. In a bloody massacre lasting less than twenty minutes, Custer and all two hundred of his men were killed. The incident became known as Custer's Last Stand. Following the battle, Sitting Bull is said to have remarked somberly, "Now the soldiers will give us no rest." He was right.

The Battle of Little Bighorn was the beginning of an era of bloody battles between whites and Indians on the western plains. Chief Crazy Horse failed to follow up on his victory. Instead, he used the next few weeks to celebrate and thank the Sioux gods for victory. He was convinced that now his people could live in peace.

But this merely gave the army time to regroup and mount a counterattack against the braves. Before long, the soldiers caught up with the Indians and chased them across the plains. One by one, the Indians were either captured or killed until there was little left of Crazy Horse's tribe. The great Sioux leader himself was finally captured and later killed by guards in an alleged attempt to escape.

Meanwhile, Chief Sitting Bull had led some of his tribe north into the safety of Canada. He returned to the Sioux reservation several years later, where he remained until he was killed when soldiers attempted to arrest him in 1890. In December of that same year, the army massacred nearly two hundred Sioux men, women, and children at Wounded Knee Creek in South Dakota. The rest of the Sioux were forced to give up their hunting grounds and the gold fields around Deadwood, South Dakota. One Sioux leader, saddened by Sitting Bull's death and the plight of his people, commented afterwards, "They [the whites] made us many promises, more than I can remember, but they never kept but one; they promised to take our land, and they took it."[3] Another, Chief Spotted Tail, remarked sadly, "Tell your people that since the Great Father [the U.S. government] promised that we should never be removed [from our lands], we have been moved five times . . . . I think you had better put the Indians on wheels and you can run them about wherever you wish."[4]

The same story of warfare followed by total Indian defeat was repeated throughout the Northwest. The Blackfoot and Crow had to leave their homes in Montana. The Apache were forced onto a reservation and several of their leaders— including the famous chief, Geronimo—died in Florida prisons. The Arapaho were forced to leave their ancestral hunting grounds in Wyoming and to resettle on an Oklahoma reservation with the Shoshoni—their traditional enemies. The Modoc managed to hold out against U.S. soldiers for six months before finally being overwhelmed and forced to surrender after a vicious battle along the border between California and Oregon.

The Nez Percé, a peaceful tribe that lived along the Salmon River in rugged Idaho and eastern Oregon, refused to surrender its land. Chief Joseph tried to avoid war, but when some of his braves were provoked into a fight with U.S. soldiers, he mounted a skillful campaign against overwhelming odds. It was one of the greatest feats in the history of Indian warfare.

After leading U.S. soldiers on a rugged chase of nearly 1,500 miles through deserts and plains, across the Yellowstone region and the Bitterroot Mountains of Montana, Chief Joseph was finally captured 30 miles south of the Canadian border, then imprisoned for a time at Leavenworth, Kansas, before being banished to the Colville Reservation in Washington.

Following his defeat, Joseph gave an eloquent speech of surrender. His story was the story of all Indians everywhere: "I am tired of fighting. Our chiefs are killed. Looking Glass is dead. Toohoolhoolzote is dead. The old men are all dead . . . I want to have time to look for my children and see how many of them I can find . . . Hear me, my chiefs! I am tired. My heart is sick and sad. From where the sun now stands, I will fight no more forever."[5]

CHAPTER THREE

NORTH TO ALASKA

Because of its location so far north of the lower forty-eight states, Alaska was settled quite differently from the rest of the northwestern United States. Many stories exist about the discovery of Alaska by white explorers. The one in which historians place the most faith centers around the Danish navigator, Vitus Bering, who made a historic voyage into the Alaskan strait that today bears his name.

Bering discovered Alaska in 1728 while working for the Russian government. When he returned to Russia to tell Czar Peter II of his discovery, the czar was too busy with Russia's domestic problems to show much interest.

Finally, in 1741, the Russian government sent Bering and a group of settlers to Alaska near modern Sitka. They were primarily traders and fur trappers who landed on present-day Kayak Island in early August. During their return trip to Russia, Bering's ship, the *St. Peter*, encountered heavy storms and fog. The ship was wrecked on November 16 on an uninhabited island. Bering, who was ill at the time of the accident, died shortly thereafter of exposure. His companions built a new vessel in which they returned to Russia with more than $100,000 worth of furs they had trapped on the island.

During the next half-century, Russia sent several groups of trappers and traders to explore the coastline of Alaska, but the first permanent settlement wasn't founded until 1784, on Kodiak Island. Before long, several other Russian trading posts had sprouted along the coast, and Alaska was beginning to take on distinctly Russian characteristics.

By the late 1700s, several other countries had sent expeditions to Alaska. The English under Captain James Cook were interested in finding a sea route from the Pacific to the Atlantic.

(opposite page)
Alaska, which lies at the northwestern tip of the U.S. mainland, is the most thinly populated state. People love to explore its vast, unspoiled wilderness.

They were also interested in obtaining trading rights with the natives. The French sent one expedition to Alaska in 1785, but their involvement in the region was cut short by the outbreak of the French Revolution in Europe in 1789.

The Spanish sent several expeditions to Alaska from Mexico to find out why the Russians were so interested in the area. But Spanish power had been dwindling in the New World for more than a century. Eventually, Spain gave up all hopes of colonizing Alaska.[1]

In 1799 a Russian fur-trading organization known as the Russian-American Company obtained exclusive rights to trade in Alaska, which was then called Russian America. Representatives of the company, led by Aleksandr Baranof, built Fort St. Michael near present-day Sitka on Baranof Island. By the early 1800s, the Russians had become the area's dominant power. But the Tlingit Indians didn't like the Russians, whom they viewed as a serious threat to their own fur-trapping and hunting activities. In 1802 the Indians attacked several Russian settlements and burned the fort to the ground. In the process, they killed many Russians and their Aleut trading partners and stole thousands of pelts. The Tlingit felt that the furs were rightfully theirs, since they had been trapped on Tlingit lands and in Tlingit waters.

Two years later, in 1804, Baranof returned to the area with a Russian armada. Russian warships bombarded the Tlingit with cannonfire while more than a hundred soldiers landed near present-day Sitka and recaptured the area. There Baranof built a new fort named New Archangel. But the Tlingit continued their raids on the Russian outposts in an attempt to win back their ancestral land.

By 1808 the Russians had built a strong working relationship with American traders who regularly stopped at Sitka to bring the Russians supplies. In return, the Americans loaded their boats with Russian furs to sell in China, where Russian ships had long been banned because of political differences between the two countries.

In time, the relationship between Russia and the United States grew strained as the American traders realized that they could make more money by trading directly with the Indians.

The relationship worsened when the Russians learned that the Americans were not only buying the Indians' furs, but also selling the Tlingit arms and ammunition with which to fight the Russians.

On September 16, 1821, Russia announced a new trade policy forbidding fur trading with foreigners. In addition, all Russian colonies in Alaska were to be supplied only by Russian ships.

The distinct design of this Eastern Orthodox Church in Juneau is living proof of the early Russian settlement of Alaska.

RUSSIA SELLS ALASKA

Russia's plan to eliminate American competition from Alaska soon backfired, as Russian colonists found themselves isolated from the American goods and services they so desperately needed. To make matters worse, the Tlingit—who were now heavily armed with American rifles—stepped up their campaign against Russian settlements. Finally, after more than a decade of dwindling profits and increasing problems with the Americans and Native Alaskans, Russia decided to sell its land holdings in Alaska. A price of $7.2 million was agreed upon, and on October 18, 1867, the United States took official possession of Alaska.

The deal had been negotiated by U.S. Secretary of State William H. Seward, who wanted Alaska for its supply of fish and fur animals. But when word of the sale reached the American public, Seward was widely criticized. Many American politicians and journalists criticized the purchase of such a cold, forbidding land. They quickly dubbed the deal "Seward's Folly," "Seward's Icebox," "Icebergia," and "Walrussia." Few Americans even knew where Alaska was. It would be more than thirty years before people would begin to realize that Seward had made one of the best land investments in the history of the United States.

GOLD!

One day, George Pilz, a German-born mining school graduate living in Sitka, got an idea. Pilz decided to finance two men in their search for gold. In 1880, Joe Juneau and Richard Harris discovered small amounts of placer (surface) gold near the Gastineau Channel in a stream they named Gold Creek. Within months, word of the find had leaked out, and hundreds of prospectors had swarmed into the area, all looking for gold. By the end of March 1881, a ship began regular monthly service, transporting people and supplies from Portland, Oregon, and Victoria, Canada, to Alaska's Harris Mining District, as the area had been named. The town that sprang up there was called Harrisburg after one of the original prospectors. In time, the miners decided to rename the city Juneau.

Within a matter of months, Juneau grew from a tiny mining outpost to a city of more than 1,200 people. Nearly all of them had three principal interests: buying, swapping, and selling gold claims. Those people who had not contracted gold fever made a fortune by selling food and supplies to those who had.

Eventually, most of the placer gold around Juneau and Gold Creek had been picked out. Then, shortly after the Juneau discovery, a Californian named John Treadwell bought a claim on Douglas Island from an old prospector named French Pete. Treadwell paid less than fifty dollars for the claim. Within weeks, he began importing heavy equipment to mine the underground deposits of the ore he was sure existed. Nearly everybody thought he was crazy. But Treadwell turned out to be right. The Treadwell Mine soon began producing large amounts of gold.

Once news of Treadwell's strike hit the nation's newspapers, the mad rush to Alaska was on once again. People quit their jobs and sold their houses to flock to the promised land. By 1884, thousands of prospectors were busy working individual claims in the hope of striking it rich. By the end of that year, those mines had yielded more than $3 million in gold. Labor grew scarce, so Treadwell soon began importing Chinese workers for his mines. Over the next five years, the mines produced so much gold that Treadwell decided to sell his mines and retire.

MORE GOLD FOUND

In 1886, shortly after the Treadwell strike, a small group of miners discovered gold around Fortymile on the American side of the Yukon River, separating eastern Alaska from Canada. In 1892, two men working in the Birch Creek area found still more precious ore. Within months, the tiny town of Circle City was booming. More than five hundred people moved to town, making it the largest settlement on the Yukon. The strike increased the yield of gold taken from the area from $30,000 in 1887 to more than $800,000 in 1896. The total value of gold extracted from Alaska that year topped $2 million.

Still the Alaska gold strikes were not over. In 1898, three men, Jafet Linden, Jon Brynteson, and Eric Lindblom—known

Prospectors line up to head over Chilkoot Pass in a frenzy to strike it rich in the Yukon Territory. In the process, Alaska would be changed forever.

as "the three Lucky Swedes"—made a large strike at Anvil Creek near Nome. Word of their strike spread quickly throughout the lower forty-eight states. Once again, the rush to Alaska was on.

The Anvil Creek strike proved to be so large that worldwide attention was focused on Alaska as never before. Even the U.S. Congress took notice. It voted money for a U.S. Geological

Survey exploration. It also extended the coal-mining laws to apply to Alaska. The U.S. Army established posts at Eagle, Nome, Haines, and elsewhere throughout the region. By 1890, Alaska had nearly doubled its population as the result of the latest gold strike.

OPENING UP THE WEST

In many ways, the discovery of gold in Alaska was similar to the great land and ranching booms in Montana and Wyoming. Once people found that money could be made quickly and easily, they flocked to the area to take advantage of the once-in-a-lifetime opportunity.

Even though most of these people failed to grow rich, the great booms played a key role in the development of the northwestern United States. They brought people into a region that previously had been overlooked. They offered people with little or no money the opportunity to earn a living. For many, they provided a new way of life, new hope for the future, and at least some degree of financial success.

But they also played a negative role in the area's development. As Alaska's white population boomed, the land that the tribes had once called home became off limits to them. The population of white settlers, which had been only 430 in 1880, leaped to more than 4,300 within ten years. Most of the migrants had come for the gold. As a result, many Native Alaskans were forced off their ancestral lands and driven east into Canada. Alaska's Native American population, which had been 32,000 in 1880, dropped to 25,000 within the same period. By 1900, whites outnumbered Native Alaskans for the first time in history—30,450 to 29,452.[2] Worse, prospectors and speculators in search of fantastic profits from Alaska's natural resources paid little attention to the rights of Native Alaskans.

Despite the fact that much of the gold being hunted was on Indian land, the lure of quick riches was so strong that public pressure eventually forced Congress to open Alaska to prospecting. The government also passed various homesteading laws similar to those in the lower forty-eight states. These laws gave land to anyone willing to live on and work it for five years.

By 1900, more than 30,000 whites were living in Nome. Two years later, a prospector named Felix Pedro discovered still more gold—this time near the present-day city of Fairbanks. Even more whites joined the mad rush to Alaska.

In order to prevent Alaska's natives from being forced off their lands entirely, Congress amended the General Allotment Act in 1906, giving each Native Alaskan family legal title to a 160-acre homestead. At first, the act sounded like a positive step. But it soon became apparent that the law actually stripped Native Alaskans of more rights than they had had before. Surviving on only 160 acres meant that a family would have to switch from hunting and food gathering to farming. But few natives knew anything about farming, and besides, Alaska's rugged land and harsh climate was ill-suited for the production of crops.

THE CREATION OF ALASKAN RESERVATIONS

Finally, in 1915, a number of Athapaskan Indian chiefs petitioned Congress to repeal the General Allotment Act. They complained about the large number of whites who were swallowing up the best of Alaska's hunting and fishing land. "When all the good land is gone . . ." the Athapaskan chiefs complained, "the Indians are going to have to move. . . ."

Congress was not swayed. Instead, it offered the natives two choices: life on 160-acre homesteads or moving to a newly created Indian reservation.

Salchaket Indian leader, Chief Joe, said: "We want to be left alone. As the whole continent was made for you [whites], God made Alaska for the Indian people, and all we hope is to be able to live here for all time."

Another Alaskan tribal leader also rejected plans to move his people to reservations. "Just as soon as you take us from the wild country and put us on reservations . . . we would all die off like rabbits. In times past, our people did not wear cotton clothes and clothes like the white man wears, but we wore skins from the caribou. We lived on fish, wild game, moose and caribou, and blueberries and roots. That is what we are made to live on—not vegetables, cattle, and things like the white people eat.

"As soon as we are made to leave our customs and wild life, we will all get sick and die. . . . You used to never hear anything of consumption or tuberculosis [European diseases]. The majority of people say that whiskey brings tuberculosis to the Indians, but this is not true. It is because we have changed our mode of living and are trying to live like the white man does."[3]

It was becoming increasingly clear to many Americans that Native Alaskans were in desperate need of help. But it would be decades before any relief would come to them through congressional action or the courts. In the meantime, they were destined to experience the same fate met by the Plains Indians—in fact, by Indians throughout the lower forty-eight states. These Indians had lived on the land for thousands of years before the coming of the first white Europeans. In a matter of centuries, nearly all of their land—and the cultures that had taken centuries to evolve—would be gone.

MANIFEST DESTINY COMES TRUE

Despite the problems created by westward expansion, America by the turn of the century stretched from sea to shining sea. Within two short years (1889 to 1890), Idaho, Montana, Wyoming, and Washington had joined Oregon as the last of the adjoining northwestern United States. Alaska, which the U.S. Senate had regarded as too small to merit statehood, was not admitted to the Union until 1959.

For many Americans, the long cherished concept of manifest destiny had finally become a reality. But the dream of uniting America from Atlantic to Pacific could never have come to pass if Americans had not found new ways of moving both people and goods quickly and easily from one coast to another. Mass transportation had finally come to America, and it played a key role in opening up the Northwest.

CHAPTER FOUR

UNITING A NATION

The bloody Civil War, which raged from 1861 to 1865, had little effect on the settlers of the Northwest except to slow down the movement of people and goods into the region. Most of the fighting took place in the southeastern and south central parts of the country—far removed from the new Northwest.

Following the war, America was once again on the move. Between 1870 and 1900, the population of the United States doubled in size. Farm production more than doubled, and the value of manufactured products grew six times. One of the main reasons for this fantastic spurt of growth was the building of the railroads. They were America's first big business, its first large-scale industry. The railroads joined the western United States with the East, brought raw materials to factories and markets around the country, and helped America to grow. At the same time, the railroads themselves were becoming huge markets for such raw materials and manufactured goods as lumber, steel, iron, and other products.

By 1862 the total number of railroad miles in the United States stood at 31,000. By 1870 that number had jumped to 53,000. During the next decade, it reached a staggering 163,000 miles. Most new railroad construction went toward filling out existing lines east of the Mississippi River, because that's where most of the nation's people lived. But the most spectacular and daring projects took place during the construction of the transcontinental railroads—long, rambling lines that stretched from the East Coast to the West.

The federal government was largely responsible for the construction of the transcontinental railroads. By 1870 federal land grants—free land given to railroads for the construction of new lines—totaled some 130 million acres. Most of this land

went to the building of the transcontinentals. In addition to federal land, the railroads received financial aid from federal, state, and local governments. This aid, according to one railroad official, reached more than $700 million in cash and $335 million in land. Without such enormous gifts, it would have cost the railroad companies too much time and money to lay tracks across the sprawling plains and through the towering mountains.

The transcontinentals got their first major push when Presi-

This is a replica of an early railroad car that ran on one of the transcontinental tracks. These railroad lines linking East to West played a major role in opening up the frontier to settlement.

dent Abraham Lincoln signed the Pacific Railway Act on July 1, 1862. The act called for the construction of a new line to be built by the Union Pacific railroad westward from Omaha, Nebraska, and by the Central Pacific railroad eastward from Sacramento. The line was to meet somewhere in between. Finally, on May 10, 1869, the two branches met at Promontory Point, Utah. The union marked a new era in American transportation, bringing settlers by the thousands to the West Coast.

Several more transcontinental lines were built in the Southwest before the first route through the Northwest was completed in 1883. This was the Northern Pacific Railroad, which connected Duluth, Minnesota, on Lake Superior with Portland, Oregon, on the coast. Ten years later, the Great Northern, which financier James J. Hill built mostly with his own money, extended from Minneapolis west through Montana's Marias Pass and on to Tacoma, Washington. By the turn of the century, a total of five transcontinental lines had cut their way through the mountains to join East with West.

RAILROADS INCREASE MARKETS

Around the time the railroads were laying track across the country, cattlemen in Texas and New Mexico were beginning to look for new markets for their beef. For years they had gathered their cattle and set out cross-country on the trip to Missouri. Dozens of hard-working cowboys drove the cattle from twelve to fourteen hours a day, seven days a week, until they reached their destination.

A typical drive usually lasted from two to three months. Along the way, the cowboys had to keep the cattle moving while protecting them from injury, disease, and thieves. Their only breaks came at mealtime, when the cowboys gathered around the chuck wagon for food—usually beef, bacon, beans, and biscuits.

(opposite page)
"Return of the Bolters," by Olaf Seltzer, paints a dramatic picture of the cowboy and his herd.

For their months of hard work, these cowboys—called drovers—usually received about a dollar a day, or half the national average wage at the time. When they finally drove their herds into the rail yards at such Kansas cow towns as Abilene, Wichita, and Kansas City, they would get paid by the trail boss. Some of the cowboys spent nearly their entire pay

gambling, drinking, and "whooping it up." When their money was gone, they simply mounted their horses and headed back to the range in search of more work. Meanwhile, the cattle would be held in huge fenced lots until they could be counted, weighed, and shipped east to market.

Although such long drives made many ranchers wealthy, the process of mounting a cattle drive was time-consuming and expensive. Ranchers soon realized that if they could graze their cattle closer to the railroads, they would not need to undertake such long and costly drives. Soon, they began eyeing the millions of acres to the north. These were the open plains of Colorado, Wyoming, and Montana. For centuries, the plains had been home to both bison and American Indians. But by the mid-1870s, most of the bison had been killed off, and the Indians had been moved to reservations. This left the area wide open for the cattle.

Since Montana and Wyoming were not yet states, the federal government owned all the open range land in the Northwest. The government, in turn, allowed ranchers to graze their cattle on the range free of charge. Before long, hundreds of ranchers from Texas, New Mexico, and Colorado were driving their cattle north to take advantage of the free range land—land just a short trail drive to the railroad centers at Ogden, Utah, and Cheyenne, Wyoming. By the early 1880s, millions of head of cattle were feeding on the open range year-round.

Cattlemen on the northwestern plains grew rich. Their herds kept growing in size while their expenses shrank. There was no fencing to maintain on the range, so the ranchers' only major expenses centered around the annual roundup and short drive to the railyards.

But by the mid-1880s, the number of cattle grazing the range had outgrown the demand for beef in the East. Beef prices began to fall. To counter falling prices, ranchers began grazing still more cattle. Before long, the grassland in many regions of the Northwest had been eaten bare.

Finally, nature delivered the cattle industry the first of a series of fatal blows. A bitter cold winter in 1885–1886 left thousands of cattle weakened or dead. The summer that followed was hot and dry. Much of the grass withered in the heat and died. Streams necessary for watering the cattle slowed to a trickle and then finally disappeared. The cattle on the range grew still thinner and weaker.

The following winter was even worse than the one before. Blizzards whipped across the open plains, piling up snow as much as ten feet high. The cattle could not reach the grass below. When the following spring came, dead cattle littered the range. More than half the cattle in Wyoming and Montana had died. Many ranchers went bankrupt.

The surviving northwestern cattlemen realized that they would have to change their ways if they were to survive in the future. They simply could not depend upon open grazing year-round anymore. They began fencing in their cattle and raising enough feed to ensure their survival through even the toughest of winters.

The role of the cowboy changed, too. Instead of riding the open range and rounding up cattle for the drive to market, he now spent most of his time digging holes for posts and stringing barbed wire to hold the cattle in.

The glory days of open range land, free-roaming cowboys, and enormous wealth were over. The Northwest was changing, and a new breed of settler was preparing to take the reins.

FARMING THE PLAINS

With the increased demand for feed, farmers with their plows and oxen began tilling the soil and planting oats, hay, and wheat. Some of them brought their own livestock to the region—mostly sheep, which require less grazing land than cattle, and dairy cattle for producing milk.

By the mid-1880s, several million people owned farms on the Great Plains. Congress helped to fuel the boom in agriculture with the passage of the Homestead Act in 1862. This act gave 160 acres of land free of charge to anyone who lived and worked on it for five years.

Thousands of Civil War veterans took advantage of the offer. Others soon followed. When word of the land giveaway reached Europe, tens of thousands of immigrants from Germany, Norway, Sweden, and other countries flooded into the region.

The railroads, too, contributed to the growth of agriculture in the Northwest, even if indirectly. They had been given hundreds of thousands of acres of land in order to lay tracks across the unsettled countryside. By the late 1880s, the railroads began selling much of their excess land to farmers.

But farmers soon found that the environment in Montana, Wyoming, and southern Idaho was far different from the farmlands they had known in the eastern United States and in Europe. The weather on the plains ranged from a scorching hot 110 degrees Fahrenheit in summer to a bone-numbing −40 degrees Fahrenheit in winter.

To make matters worse, rainfall ranged from little to next to none. The sun-baked topsoil was so tough that ordinary iron plows quickly snapped in two. There were few trees on the plains from which to build houses and fences sturdy enough to keep livestock out of the fields, and without fences, free-ranging cattle could trample a farmer's crops to the ground within hours.

FARMERS LEARN TO ADAPT

Farmers on the plains realized they would have to adapt to the harsh conditions of the Northwest if they were to survive. Two inventions helped them to become successful. One was a new type of plow made of extra-strong iron. The new plow was able to cut through the tough prairie sod quickly and easily.

The second was barbed wire, a type of wire with sharp points, or barbs, woven into it every few inches. The barbs discouraged cattle from leaning against and breaking the wire. The new wire allowed farmers to build fences with a minimum of wood. A single wooden post every six feet or so was sufficient. As a result, the demand for barbed wire on the plains grew so fast that one factory was soon producing more than six hundred miles of wire a day!

Neither of these two inventions could help the farmers with the weather, though. Locked into an area with little rainfall and few running streams or rivers, farmers on the plains eventually developed a system known as dry farming. They dug narrow furrows, or ditches, on each side of a row of crops. These furrows collected dew and rain and held it in one spot until the plants' roots had a chance to absorb it.

Farmers also began switching from crops that required large amounts of water to those that needed much less, like certain varieties of wheat, oats, and hay. These crops grew well under the relentless pounding of the sun and brought in the cash that farmers needed for survival.

Farmers encountered some problems, though, that they were helpless to prevent. Among the worst were grasshoppers. These destructive pests appeared every few years and attacked farmers' crops, eating every plant in sight. At times, the insects were so thick that they actually blocked out the sun and darkened the sky. A farmer could have hundreds of acres of hay or corn one day and nothing but empty fields the next. One

By the end of the 1800s, livestock farms, such as this one with its fenced-in cattle, pigs, and sheep, began to replace the early open-range farms of the Wild West.

farmer wrote: "So thick were the grasshoppers in the cornfield . . . that not a spot of green could be seen. And within two hours of the time they had come, not a leaf was left in all that field."[1]

Despite problems such as insects, drought, and unstable farm prices, farmers on the plains somehow managed to survive and prosper. By the early 1900s, ranching began staging a comeback. Slow but steady increases in beef prices, combined with new ranching techniques to improve the genetic quality of cattle, played a key role in this revival.

CHAPTER FIVE

THE GROWING NORTHWEST

By the early 1900s, the Industrial Revolution in the East and the Midwest was placing a severe strain on the nation's supply of raw materials, such as coal, oil, gas, and various metals. The northwestern states soon found themselves in a unique position to furnish the nation with the materials it needed for heavy industry. Strip mining, which removes large areas of soil to expose coal and metal ore, soon spread from one end of the Northwest to the other. By the mid-1900s, mining had taken over as the number-one industry in the region. Coal, copper, silver, gold, uranium, and other valuable materials were soon flowing from Montana, Wyoming, Idaho, and eastern Oregon.

Although strip mines proved to be safer and cheaper to operate than the deep underground mines of the eastern and south central United States, they also proved to be extremely damaging to the environment, polluting the land, air, and water. Since the early 1960s, strip mines have increasingly come under fire from environmentalists who have been working to halt pollution. As a result, some strip mines have been closed down, while others have adopted various antipollution measures. The remaining mines provide thousands of jobs and produce millions of dollars of revenue for the Northwest each year.

THE GROWTH OF THE NORTHWESTERN CITIES

While most of the cities on the northwestern plains were being built on the fortunes of ranching and mining, several of the region's coastal cities, such as Portland, Oregon, and Seattle, Washington, grew up around trade, commercial fishing, logging, and related industries. In Seattle, Boeing Industries grew into a major international company dedicated to producing airplanes and, later, aerospace components. The company eventually became the largest single employer of people in the Pacific Northwest. Meanwhile, the coming of World War II provided motivation for Oregon to expand Portland as a key port for shipping supplies to American naval and military forces stationed in the Pacific.

Yet, Portland found itself limited in economic growth by its surrounding natural topography. Unlike the northeastern coastline, which is strewn with natural deepwater harbors, the only natural shelter in the entire Northwest runs from Tacoma, Washington, north into the straits of Juan de Fuca and Georgia and, from there, to Vancouver, Canada.

Even the mouth of the Columbia River, one hundred miles downstream from Portland, is guarded by dangerous shoals and treacherous waves. The waters off Cape Disappointment—named because they failed to lead to a passage to the Atlantic Ocean—are so unpredictable that the largest grain ships wouldn't dare sail them fully loaded, and oil supertankers are simply out of the question. Shipping into and out of Portland is mostly limited to small and mid-sized ships or larger ships only partially loaded with cargo.[1]

ALASKA STRUGGLES AGAINST THE ODDS

Meanwhile, Alaska has continued to struggle over bitter disputes involving the commercial development of its land. At the center of these battles have been the Native Alaskans.

In 1944, the Tlingit and Haida tribes—two of Alaska's largest—filed suit against the U.S. government for $35 million "for the value of the land, hunting, and fishing rights taken without compensation" by the U.S. government. The suit was quickly thrown out of court because the Tlingit's lawyers had not been approved by the secretary of the interior, as legal actions involving Native Americans require.

The Tlingit and Haida soon filed another suit, and in 1959 the Court of Claims found that the government had taken Alaskan tribal land without just payment. The government appealed the decision, with court action dragging on for the next nine years. Finally, the Court of Appeals upheld the initial

(opposite page)
Alaska has a booming fishing industry. Disputes between whites and Indians over fishing rights have raged for many years. Here, salmon is hung to dry after a good catch.

court's findings. On January 9, 1969, the Tlingit and Haida were awarded compensation of more than $7 million and two million acres of land.

In the meantime, Alaska's economy was shifting its focus from fishing and trading to something far more profitable—oil production. In 1957 the Richfield Oil Company (which became Atlantic Richfield in 1966) made a large oil strike at the Swanson River on the Kenai Peninsula. The company sank two wells during the next two years. It also discovered a large reserve of offshore oil in Alaska's Cook Inlet. There, newly drilled oil and gas fields were soon producing fossil fuel for an energy-hungry America.

Afraid that they would be left out of sharing in the huge profits from the oil finds, the Indians began forming statewide native organizations to protect their economic interests. Then, in 1968, massive deposits of oil were discovered at Prudhoe Bay in the Arctic. Atlantic Richfield, British Petroleum, and Humble Oil submitted an application to the U.S. Department of the Interior to build a pipeline to carry the oil from Prudhoe Bay to Prince William Sound, a distance of nearly eight hundred miles. From there, the oil would be loaded on ships and taken to markets around the world.

The pipeline proposal created a national furor. The oil companies pressured Congress to build the pipeline because of the huge profits they knew it would bring them. Many Alaskans wanted the pipeline for the jobs and much-needed boost to the state's economy it would bring. But environmentalists feared that building the pipeline through some of Alaska's most sensitive ecological regions would destroy valuable wildlife habitat.

Early in 1970, Secretary of the Interior Walter J. Hickel announced that he had decided to issue a permit for construction of the pipeline. But that March, five Indian villages asked the federal district court in Washington, D.C., to issue an injunction stopping Hickel from issuing the permit. The Indians based their request on their claim that the land over which the pipeline would pass belonged to them. The court issued a temporary order stopping all construction.

British Petroleum—one of the pipeline's major proponents—realized that a pipeline would never be built until the question of Indian rights was settled. The company decided to join the Indians and pressure Congress for a law that would return legal ownership of the land to the tribes.

After nearly a year and a half of debates, the Alaska Federation of Natives (AFN), organized in 1967, was granted legal ownership to 44 million acres of Alaskan land. They were also given money totaling nearly $1 billion. On December 18, 1971, President Richard M. Nixon signed the measure into law. Under the law, all U.S. citizens who were at least one quarter Native Alaskan were entitled to benefit from the land sale. Each native would become a stockholder, or part owner, in the new pipeline corporation. The law also placed up to 80 million acres of Alaskan land into national parks or forests, wildlife refuges, and wild and scenic river systems for protection from future commercial development.

As a result of the law, neither the Native Alaskans nor the state of Alaska would ever again be the same. The Native Alaskans had surrendered many of their ancient rituals and ways of life. In return, they received a big boost into twentieth-century American society.

THE NORTHWEST TODAY

Today, the American Northwest remains a sparsely settled mix of commerce and industry. Partly because it was the last area of the United States to be settled and partly because of its rugged, mountainous terrain, the region has fewer people, fewer large cities, and fewer economic opportunities than any other part of the country.

But what the northwestern United States lacks in these areas it more than makes up for in beauty. From the open plains of eastern Montana and Wyoming to the majestic Rocky Mountains, from the roaring Snake River of Idaho to the thick carpets of pine and cedar in Washington and Oregon, from the hundreds of islands of Washington's Puget Sound to the millions of acres of unspoiled beauty of Alaska, the Northwest is one of the most beautiful and least spoiled regions in the world.

The pioneer spirit still lives in the American Northwest. Prospectors still hunt for gold among the mountains and streams. Ranchers still graze their cattle on unfenced land that

seems to roll on forever. Fishermen still head to sea in search of bountiful harvests.

Yet, despite the millions of people each year who flock to the region in search of dude ranches and whitewater river trips, for hunting, fishing, and taking in the natural beauty of Yellowstone Park, the Northwest remains set apart from the rest of the country. Residents of Juneau, Alaska—the state's thriving capital—still must enter or leave the city by air or sea. No road has yet been built to service the city.

Despite the hardships that such terrain offers, or perhaps because of them, most residents of the region are in awe of the area's natural beauty and would never choose to live anywhere else.

(opposite page)
*A farm in Oregon.
Despite the growing
population in the
Northwest, much of
the region retains a
quiet, rural feel.*

A P P E N D I X

STATE FIRSTS

ALASKA   Statehood: 1959

Alaska was the site of the earliest migration of Asians into the Americas around 15,000 years ago. These early Asians eventually evolved into Alaska's Tlingit, Tinnes, Aleut, and Eskimos.

Russia's Peter the Great sponsored the first expedition to find land east of Siberia in 1728. Thirteen years later, Vitus Bering landed near present-day Mount St. Elias and began the first fur-trading business with Europe and Asia.

The Russians established the first permanent European settlement at Three Saints Bay near present-day Kodiak in 1784.

Gold was discovered near the Stikine River in 1861, Juneau in 1880, Nome in 1898, and Fairbanks in 1903. The discoveries set off one of the wildest gold rushes in American history.

IDAHO   Statehood: 1890

After crossing the Bitterroot Mountains, the explorers Meriwether Lewis and William Clark reached Idaho in August 1805. They camped on the site of present-day Lewiston before continuing on their journey to the Pacific Ocean.

The first irrigation ditches were dug in Idaho by the Mormons in 1855. As a result, millions of acres of desert land have been changed over the years into productive cropland.

MONTANA   Statehood: 1889

At St. Mary's Mission, wheat and potatoes were planted by Jesuit missionary Father De Smet in 1842. Three years later, the first gristmill was built by Father Ravelli. Today, Montana is a leading wheat-growing state.

In 1864, John M. Bozeman and a train of wagons left for the gold fields over a new trail from Fort Laramie, Wyoming. Gold was discovered in Montana on Gold Creek in 1852 and later at Bannack (1862), near Virginia City (1863), and near Helena (1864).

Oil was discovered in 1864 when an army wagon rumbling over a mountain road struck a boulder and broke a wheel. The driver went looking for water and discovered an oil-covered pool, from which he filled his grease can. Production of petroleum began in 1915.

In 1896, a sheepherder gathered up a handful of attractive blue pebbles from a gopher hole—the first discovery of the area's sapphires. The mountains of Montana also hold large quantities of rubies and garnets.

OREGON   Statehood: 1859

Meriwether Lewis and William Clark established Fort Clatsop near present-day Astoria during the winter of 1805–1806, following their remarkable journey across the continent from St. Louis.

Oregon lumber was first used for building pioneer homes and sailing ships after 1841, when the *Star of Oregon* was launched. The invention of the steam-driven circular saw allowed lumber mills to greatly increase their output.

In 1937 the Bonneville Dam and lock, begun in 1933, was completed forty miles east of Portland. The dam deepened the Columbia River to allow ships to sail as far upstream as The Dalles. It also provided hydroelectricity for the region. Special fish ladders were built to allow the salmon to work their way upstream to spawn.

WASHINGTON   Statehood: 1889

American captain Robert Gray discovered the Columbia River, which he named after his ship, the *Columbia*.

In the fall of 1805, the Lewis and Clark expedition reached the Pacific Northwest after crossing the Rocky Mountains and traveling down the Snake and Columbia rivers to the coast.

In 1810, the North West Company established the Spokane House, a fur-trading post that eventually became the first permanent white settlement in the state.

In the 1860s, the first canneries were built on the Columbia River, and the salmon-canning industry was born. Before that time, salmon had been preserved by salting or smoking.

WYOMING   Statehood: 1890

In 1807, trapper John Colter discovered a scenic area of Wyoming, and in 1872, the U.S. government established Yellowstone National Park "for the benefit and enjoyment of the people." It was the first of the nation's national parks.

In 1832, Captain Benjamin de Bonneville and a company of soldiers cut the first wagon route across the Rockies to the Green River by way of the South Pass. This was the same route used by those who would rush to the California gold fields in the 1850s.

Wyoming was the first state to offer women the right to vote in 1869—some fifty-one years before getting the right elsewhere in the United States. In 1870, Esther H. Morris of South Pass City became the first woman justice of the peace in the United States, and in 1924, Nellie Tayloe Ross was elected the first woman governor.

NOTES

CHAPTER ONE
THE INDIANS OF THE NORTHWEST

1. Clark Wissler, *Indians of the United States* (New York: Anchor Books, 1989), p. 284.

CHAPTER TWO
WESTWARD HO!

1. Herbert J. Bass, *People in Time and Place* (Morristown, N.J.: Silver Burdett & Ginn, 1991), pp. 376–377.
2. Ibid, p. 475.
3. Richard H. Dillon, *North American Indian Wars* (New York: Facts on File, Inc., 1983), p. 251.
4. George Brown Tindall, *America: A Narrative History* (New York: W. W. Norton & Company, 1984), p. 732.
5. Ibid, p. 734.

CHAPTER THREE
NORTH TO ALASKA

1. Claus M. Naske and Herman E. Slotnick, *Alaska: A History of the 49th State* (Norman, Okla.: University of Oklahoma Press, 1987), pp. 31–32.
2. Ibid, pp. 187–188.
3. Ibid, p. 189.

CHAPTER FOUR
UNITING A NATION

1. Bass, *People in Time and Place*, p. 484.

CHAPTER FIVE
THE GROWING NORTHWEST

1. Joel Garreau, *The Nine Nations of North America* (Boston: Houghton Mifflin Company, 1981), pp. 258–259.

SELECTED BIBLIOGRAPHY

Bass, Herbert J. *People in Time and Place*. Morristown, N.J.: Silver Burdett & Ginn, 1991.

Casner, Mabel B., and Ralph H. Gabriel. *Story of the American Nation*. New York: Harcourt, Brace & World, Inc., 1962.

Gutman, Herbert G. *Who Built America?* New York: Pantheon Books, 1989.

Schaefer, Richard T. *Racial and Ethnic Groups*. Glenview, Ill.: Scott, Foresman and Company, 1990.

Tindall, George Brown. *America: A Narrative History*. New York: W. W. Norton & Company, 1984.

Wissler, Clark. *Indians of the United States*. New York: Anchor Books, 1989.

Wright, John W., ed. *The Universal Almanac*. Kansas City: Universal Press Syndicate, 1990.

SUGGESTED READING

Aylesworth, Thomas G., and Virginia L. Aylesworth. *The Northwest*. New York: Chelsea House, 1992.

Behrens, June. *A New Flag for a New Country*. Chicago, Ill.: Childrens Press, 1975.

Billington, Ray Allen. *Westward Expansion: A History of the American Frontier*. New York: Macmillan Publishing Co., 1974.

Dillon, Richard H. *North American Indian Wars*. New York: Facts on File, 1983.

Freedman, Russell. *Indian Chiefs*. New York: Holiday House, 1987.

Smith, Carter, ed. *A Sourcebook on the American West: Bridging the Continent*. Brookfield, Conn.: The Millbrook Press, 1992.

————. *A Sourcebook on the American West: Exploring the Frontier*. Brookfield, Conn.: The Millbrook Press, 1992.

————. *A Sourcebook on the American West: Native Americans of the West*. Brookfield, Conn.: The Millbrook Press, 1992.

————. *A Sourcebook on the American West: The Riches of the West*. Brookfield, Conn.: The Millbrook Press, 1992.

INDEX